A prototype Land-Rover: a version from about 1965 of the lightweight air-portable model that entered service in 1968. In production there were minor changes, including the substitution of a standard wire grille. The weight had been pared down to enable the fully laden vehicle to be carried by a Westland Wessex helicopter.

FOUR-WHEEL DRIVE AND LAND-ROVER

Nick Baldwin

Shire Publications Ltd

CONTENTS

Published in 2001 by Shire Publications Ltd, Cromwell House, Church Street, Princes Risborough, Buckinghamshire HP27 9AA, UK. Copyright © 1988 and 2001 by Nick Baldwin. First published 1988. Second edition 1997. Third edition 2001. Shire Album 221. ISBN 0 7478 0509 1.

Printed in Great Britain by CIT Printing Services Ltd, Press Buildings, Merlins Bridge, Haverfordwest, Pembrokeshire SA61 1XF.

British Library Cataloguing in Publication Data: Baldwin, Nick. Four-wheel drive and Land-Rover. – 3rd ed. (Shire album; no. 221) 1. Four-wheel drive vehicles – History. 2. Four-wheel drive vehicles – Pictorial works. I. Title. 629.2'2042. ISBN 0 7478 0509 1.

Editorial Consultant: Michael E. Ware, former Director of the National Motor Museum, Beaulieu.

ACKNOWLEDGEMENTS
The pictures are mostly from the author's collection and in many cases originally came from the vehicle manufacturers concerned. The Rover Group deserves special thanks, as does David Shephard, who took the cover photograph and helped in other ways. The excellent library at the National Motor Museum, Beaulieu, provided invaluable assistance in writing the captions.

Cover: *One of the first: a Land-Rover 1948 model owned and restored by Andrew Stevens.*

Below: *Various ways were tried to give 4 x 2 vehicles adequate off-road potential in the early years of the twentieth century. B. J. Diplock studied elephants before making his Pedrail wheel, shown here on a steam traction engine.*

This is said to be a 4 x 4 Spyker of 1904, photographed at Brighton in 1905. It has the typical features of the Dutch car, including the elaborate dust shields under the chassis and the circular radiator and bonnet with louvres. Although the shields and rear competition number make it difficult to see details of the transmission, there is certainly a live axle as opposed to chain drive at the rear.

THE ORIGINS OF FOUR-WHEEL DRIVE

We are all familiar with the transmission arrangements of the average family car. Its engine drives either the front or rear wheels via a differential, which allows one wheel to turn more or fewer revolutions than its mate when cornering. Without the differential each driven wheel would skid to compensate for the different distance that it had to cover on a corner when compared with the wheel attached to the other end of its axle. Whilst the differential is invaluable on hard surfaces, on soft ones it effectively makes a car have only one-wheel drive because all the power tends to go to the wheel that is meeting the least resistance : in other words the wheel that is spinning helplessly.

Four-wheel drive (4 x 4) is a straightforward system of feeding the engine power to both front and rear wheels by revolving shafts. (The original military term '4 x 4' implied four wheels, all four driven, double-tyred wheels counting as one.)

However, as in the case of two-wheel drive (4 x 2) vehicles, it is possible for one wheel to spin on each axle and effectively immobilise the vehicle. To avoid this happening some 4 x 4s have differentials that can be locked to force equal power to all wheels. Many 4 x 4s can be driven on the road as 4 x 2s, which indeed they need to be if there is no differential between the shafts driving the front and rear axles. The explanation for this is that, just as wheels on opposite sides of a car travel different distances, so do the front and rear wheels. Thus, a vehicle in permanent four-wheel drive with no central differential would soon scuff its tyres bald. A third differential might permit all the power to go to the least resistance and make just one wheel spin, so once more a lock is provided. With all the differentials locked solid a 4 x 4 becomes genuinely four-wheel drive and is virtually unstoppable.

One tends to think of four-wheel drive

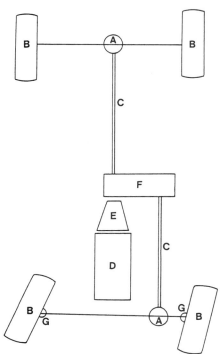

Four-wheel drive. A, Housing for gearing to provide right-angle distribution of power and containing a differential (sometimes lockable). B, Wheels: note that the front ones adopt different angles when steered. C, Propellor shafts. D, Engine. E, Gearbox. F, Transfer box giving option of 4 x 2 or 4 x 4 or else containing a third differential and providing permanent 4 x 4. Usually a second ratio is built into the transfer box to provide crawler gears for slow off-road use. G, Constant velocity joints to allow simultaneous drive and steering.

as stemming from the Second World War. This was when all-wheel drive first came into widespread use but the origins of four-wheel drive date back to the dawn of motoring. Burstall and Hill's steam carriage, built in Leith in 1825, had optional four-wheel drive and the famous French designer Amedée Bollée took up the idea fifty years later. Gandon built a 4 x 4 steam lorry in Paris in 1900 and internal combustion-engined examples achieved fame in 1903 with the remarkable Spyker racing car from Holland.

Until then four-wheel drive had been used simply to increase traction on rough tracks and fields: after all, very few proper roads existed. Even in 1914 only 3296 miles of North American roads had hard surfaces, compared with over two million without. The Spyker, however, was intended for metalled roads and four-wheel drive was chosen to ensure that the power from its 8.7 litre, six-cylinder engine was put to maximum use when accelerating and cornering.

It was to be fifty years before these matters were to be considered seriously again by designers. In the meantime it was off-road ability or the need to keep vehicles moving in snow and mud that took priority. Most interest was shown in the United States. Battery electric 4 x 4 trucks were available from Couple Gear and Quadray in 1904; these makers soon added petrol-engined generators to increase range. However, it was to the Badger that most early credit goes, despite the fact that the Duplex, in Badger's home state of Wisconsin, may have been a little earlier.

German immigrants William A. Besserdich and Otto Zachow built a steam-driven 4 x 4 car in 1908 and then built a 45 horsepower Continental four-cylinder petrol-engined Badger in 1909. It could carry seven passengers at up to 55 mph (89 km/h) on good surfaces yet crawl through quagmires impossible for all but light horse-drawn vehicles. It had the advantage of four-wheel braking via the transmission at a time when the vast majority of cars had only two-wheel brakes. It also had double reduction axles and a third differential that eliminated wind-up in the transmission between front and rear axles. This differential could be locked if the ground conditions became difficult.

Ten of these cars were built by Badger, which had become the Four Wheel Drive Auto Company. FWD was soon to find true success in the field of trucks, but not before it had sold one of its 1912 cars to Mr Pinkerton of the famous detective agency.

Similar to the FWD forward-control truck, but with the addition of steering on all wheels, was the Rambler (later Jeffery and then Nash) Quad which appeared in Wisconsin in 1913 and by a tenuous route of company changes of ownership was to be an ancestor of the Jeep. Another early American maker was Walter, whose first 4 x 4 appeared in 1911 and whose name still

Petrol-engined Badger cars were built in Clintonville, Wisconsin, United States, from 1909 by the forerunner of the Four Wheel Drive Auto Company. This is the first, still preserved at the firm's museum. It had the nickname of 'The Battleship' because it was nearly unstoppable.

A petrol-electric bus in use in Vienna in 1911. It had Lohner-Porsche electric motors in four wheels, which made it ideal for towing the passenger trailer in icy and snowy conditions. Note the chute for sand to help the solid-tyred rear wheels grip.

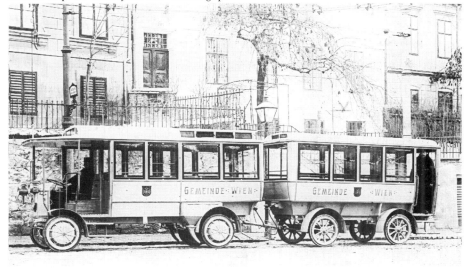

Britain was generally slow to adopt four-wheel drive, partly because its railway communications were so good and partly because many roads had hard surfaces. However, the technology existed, as this 20 horsepower Standard, built for the Delhi Durbah of 1913, goes to prove.

exists on snow-ploughs and crash tenders for airfields.

Meanwhile, in Europe Georges Latil of Marseilles had developed in 1898 a driven front axle that was used initially for attachment to existing horse-drawn vehicles. From this it was but a relatively small step to add drive to the rear axle as well. Exactly when this took place is uncertain but 4 x 4 Latils were in widespread use during the First World War. These Latils were shaft-driven but Ferdinand Porsche developed a system in 1898 which employed separate electric motors in each wheel and thus simplified the transmission of power.

Germany and Austria favoured four-wheel drive for military purposes and as early as 1905 Austro-Daimler was offering heavy gun tractors with all-wheel drive. In 1906 German Daimler made shaft-driven 4 x 4 tractors and lorries, in 1907 Mercedes made a large 4 x 4 car for use in Africa and in 1910 Ehrhardt made a 4 x 4 gun carriage. From 1911 Chatillon-Panhard made gun tractors in France and in Australia the Caldwell Vale Motor and Tractor Construction Company made forty massive 4 x 4 lorries from 1910 to 1912 for the peaceful purpose of opening up the outback.

Equally pacific in intention was the fleet of 4 x 4 cars built by Standard of Coventry for use on a royal visit to the Delhi Durbah in 1913. Based on the 20 horsepower high-ground-clearance Colonial Standard, they looked just like normal touring cars until the drive to the centre of the front axle was noted.

Though the Standards were light enough to use pneumatic tyres, most of the heavier types of 4 x 4 vehicle had iron or solid rubber tyres, which inevitably limited their grip. To overcome this they used strakes or chains when working in soft conditions.

Probably the first heavier 4 x 4 truck to make pneumatic tyres standard, in 1917, was the vehicle that became known as the Oshkosh. It was made by William Besser-

In 1898 Georges Latil developed a self-contained front-wheel drive power pack which was originally coupled to existing vehicles. Soon complete front-wheel drive or four-wheel drive vehicles were built for him by Ets Charles Blum at Levallois and tractors by Ets Tourand. This is a 1913-14 example.

dich after he left FWD in 1913. At that early stage he was beginning to despair that four-wheel drive would ever be commercially viable. The total of six FWD cars and five trucks sold in 1912 had been disheartening, and the total of nineteen trucks in 1913 was little better. A surprise order for fifty trucks for the British Army came too late to influence William Besser-dich's move. Subsequent output by FWD in the war years 1914-18 was a remarkable fifteen thousand vehicles.

The Italian Pavesi was developed in the First World War and was subsequently adopted by Fiat. At first it had a two-cylinder engine but it had acquired a four-cylinder unit by the time that this one (shown with snow-plough blade) was built in the mid 1920s. Because it pivoted in the middle in order to steer, the wheels followed each other's tracks and the machine was virtually unstoppable, particularly when strakes were fitted to the rims.

In 1923 French's Motor Engineering Works in London built this Anzani-engineered 4 x 4 with Wrigley gearbox to the design of a Belgian named Hollé. It could steer on all wheels and employed a central transfer box from which four shafts passed direct to bevel gearing in each wheel hub. Little more was heard of the ingenious vehicle until 1926 when Vulcan made a larger Hoverta Vulcan version.

THE FIRST WORLD WAR AND AFTER

During the First World War 4 x 4 vehicles were used extensively for the first time. They were used for carrying supplies and troops and for towing guns in the appalling conditions of mud and destroyed roads. Germany and its allies tended to use four-wheel drive for their largest vehicles, whereas Italy, France and the United States made relatively lightweight and manoeuvrable 4 x 4s. One of the most interesting designs emanated from the Italian Ing Pavesi and consisted of a two-cylinder, short wheelbase machine which steered by pivoting the two halves of its frame in the middle. It was a universal pivot that also allowed the wheels to keep in even contact with the ground, however bumpy. Fiat ultimately took over this design.

French makers like Latil, Renault and Panhard made relatively small numbers of vehicles because of the conflict within their country and Britain concentrated on producing as many conventional 4 x 2 three-tonners as it could. As a result it was left to FWD, and its licensees, as well as the variously named Quads and lesser rivals, to fill the breach. Tens of thousands were delivered, despite early problems when some of the inhabitants of Wisconsin, long a favoured state for German immigrants, did their own bit for the war effort by sabotaging the 4 x 4s being sent to the Allies in Europe.

When the war ended many military vehicles went on to serve civilian functions and for a long time an industry existed in England (FWD at Slough) and France (Labourier) reconditioning 4 x 4 chassis and fitting them with new equipment like

Most requirements for off-road vehicles in the 1920s were met by 6 x 4 designs. Above is a Renault staff car with twin tyres all round for extra flotation on sand. Another way of improving off-road capabilities is shown by the Morris-Commercial (below) converted to half-tracks by Roadless Traction.

Above: *An American FWD of First World War origin shown in service in London in the 1920s. The FWD was an important design which met most needs for off-road civilian vehicles in the 1920s in Europe and America. Note the original wooden wheels: these were gradually replaced by steel types on FWDs in Britain.*

Below: *The first Oshkosh of 1917, made in the town of that name in Wisconsin, USA, is dwarfed by another all-wheel drive Oshkosh, a J series 6 x 6 tractor built for desert use in the 1970s.*

tipper bodies and snow-ploughs (and ultimately building substitutes from new components). The Latil, with four-wheel drive and four-wheel steering, as well as the Pavesi, went on to serve as timber winches and tractors. Most other new types of 4 x 4 vehicle were effectively stifled by the wartime surplus.

Thornycroft, in England, made a few 4 x 4 Hathis in the mid 1920s and Scammell offered all-wheel drive later in the decade, but most emphasis shifted to 6 x 4, a cheaper and simpler way of providing useful off-road capability. For even more difficult conditions half-tracks at the back of cars and lorries were developed by several firms, notably by Roadless Traction in England.

Little attention was paid to light 4 x 4 vehicles, though a most ingenious design from a Belgian named Hollé was built experimentally by French's Motor Engineering Works in London in 1923. It had an Anzani engine and a central transfer box from which four drive shafts radiated direct to each wheel, all of which steered. The idea was taken up in the Holverta Vulcan of 1926 and was later seen in certain Italian 4 x 4s.

Unfortunately there was little commercial demand for 4 x 4 vehicles, which were inevitably relatively costly and complicated. Military demand was minimal and, though undeveloped territories were being opened up overseas, it was to 6 x 4s and half-tracks that most of the work was entrusted. The British Colonial Office had come to an arrangement with 23 countries to share the cost of some off-road trains in 1927. These were hauled by Leyland and AEC 8 x 8 tractors, but few were built, it proving more economic in the longer term to use aircraft or to build proper roads or railways.

Gun tractors and lorries were made by several firms for Germany and its allies in the period leading up to and during the First World War. This is one of Ferdinand Porsche's designs on test in 1914. It could tow a 30.5 cm Mauser and had an 80 bhp engine.

Marmon-Herrington's all-wheel driven vehicles were often Ford-based, as in the case of this personnel carrier made for Persia. The firm was run by Colonel Herrington and the brother of the maker of Marmon luxury cars. By using cheap and freely available components they were able to bring four-wheel drive within reach of many new customers.

THE 1930s AND SECOND WORLD WAR

The 1930s commenced with interest in all-wheel drive at a low ebb. The world economic recession favoured the production of cheap and basic vehicles and this was the era of widespread mass production of standard motor cars. Specialist firms eked out an existence with orders for road-building, snow-ploughing and cable-laying vehicles and cheap, light cross-country vehicles tended to be of the half-track variety typified by the Citroen-Kegresse.

In an effort to provide competitively priced 4 x 4 vehicles in the United States, Colonel Arthur W. Herrington began to convert Fords. His firm, Marmon-Herrington, started with heavier types in 1931, using the former Duesenberg factory for production. The Ford conversions became big business in 1936: by then re-armament in the United States and Europe was causing increased interest in many types of off-road vehicle. The Latil 4 x 4 had remained in production in France and in Britain the local FWD firm had been acquired by AEC. A direct descendant of the reworked American FWDs would ultimately become one of the most famous vehicles of the Second World War: the AEC Matador.

In Italy Fiat acquired most of its competitors, amongst which was OM, which had itself acquired an outstanding 4 x 4 from Ansaldo in 1932. This was the Autocarro designed by Giulio Cesare Cappa in 1928 and sometimes called the Autocarretta da Montagna. It had a 1.6 litre, two-cylinder, air-cooled engine, independent suspension and four-wheel steering. It was a far cleverer design than that of the famous Jeep, though this received most of the credit for pioneering four-wheel drive in a lightweight form.

Before considering the Jeep it is important to recall that Germany was keenly interested in 4 x 4 cars in the 1930s. Its rearmament was of a rather circumspect nature and, to keep off-road technology high on the agenda without being too overtly military, all manner of cross-country car trials were organised. The fact that the average car club member stood no chance of achieving success unless he had been loaned a special 4 x 4 seemed to have been overlooked by the Allies. In theory the Tempo G1200 was freely available from 1936 and is said to have been sold to some forty countries. Stoewer made a clever 4 x 4 with all-wheel steering and, when this was taken up by the Wehrmacht, BMW and Hanomag helped with its production. Wanderer in the Auto Union group made ingenious six-cylinder 4 x 4 cars from 1933, as did the sister firm of Horch, using eight-cylinder engines.

In the 1930s Mercedes-Benz was one of the most prolific suppliers of both 6 x 4 and 4 x 4 cars, most of the latter having all-wheel steering. Even Japan, which was slow to become a motor manufacturer, built 4 x 4 cars for military purposes. The Mitsubishi PX-33 of 1934 was remarkable in being diesel-powered. Its engine was a six-cylinder 70 bhp unit displacing 4390 cc.

Whilst Marmon-Herrington was stealing the limelight in America, the traditional firms like Walter, Oshkosh and FWD continued to make small numbers of vehicles. As a publicity exercise FWD raced a Miller-engined 4 x 4 car at the Indianapolis 500 between 1932 and 1937. Qualifying speeds of up to 118.4 mph (191 km/h) were recorded but no victories were scored. Even so, it provided a valuable lesson in torque proportioning differentials and constant velocity transmission joints.

The big 4 x 4 event in America at the end of the decade was the emergence of Karl Probst's Bantam. American Austin

Scammell emerged as one of Britain's principal producers of specialist heavy vehicles from the late 1920s. It made several types of 4 x 4 and 6 x 6 vehicles and here one shows off the drive to its front axle and the considerable degree of flexibility allowed by the centrally mounted transverse leaf spring.

There was much interest in off-road trials in Germany during the 1930s and most of the country's manufacturers built 4 x 4 cars. Shown here is one from Auto Union (the controlling group for Wanderer, Audi and DKW) being driven by a Nazi Party member (note the swastika armband), aided by a navigator who clung on to straps at the rear to improve traction.

had built the immortal Seven under licence and the US Army had even tested these as scout cars in 1933. The firm had a chequered career, becoming American Bantam in 1936. The Continental-engined 4 x 4 did well in its military trial and 2675 examples were built in 1940-1. Bantam was far too small to make the vast numbers required and mass production of similar vehicles was left to Ford and Willys-Overland. Known as General Purpose vehicles, the initials GP were soon corrupted to Jeep, a familiar character in the Popeye cartoons.

By the end of the war approximately 740,000 Jeeps had been produced. Their mark on motoring history is inestimable because many of these, plus new civilian versions, went on after the war to fill roles that had never before been dreamed of. Their European predecessors and contemporaries were mostly far more complex and therefore more expensive to produce and maintain. As a result they were built in much smaller quantities and had far less impact on the subsequent civilian market.

However, large types of 4 x 4 vehicle produced by General Motors and Ford in Canada and by General Motors' offshoot

Bedford in Britain also had great significance. These were, again, simple no-frills vehicles and hundreds of thousands were ultimately in use, of which no less than 52,245 were the ubiquitous Bedford QL 3 ton model. Bedford had never before made a forward-control vehicle, let alone a 4 x 4, so its achievements were remarkable, even though partly counteracted by the fact that General Motors' Opel factory had been taken over by the German government to make equally potent Opel Blitz lorries.

The Second World War marked a major turning point for 4 x 4. Time and time again all-wheel driven vehicles showed their superiority over conventional machines and henceforth a high proportion of military vehicles would have 4 x 4, 6 x 6 or even 8 x 8. Many of the duties formerly performed by tracked vehicles were now undertaken by wheeled machines. Though in the 1930s most interest had been towards military ends, four-wheel drive had also proved itself to be useful in opening up desert and forest regions in the search for raw materials. This was to be an area of massive expansion in the coming years.

Right: *Britain made few small 4 x 4 vehicles before the arrival of the Land-Rover. One exception was the wartime Humber Heavy Utility. This was based on Super Snipe mechanical components where possible and used its 4.08 litre, 85 bhp engine. The gearbox was a two-range four-speed unit and there was independent suspension at the front.*

Left: *The original Jeep was perhaps the most famous light 4 x 4 of all time. Following the successful prototype at American Bantam, versions built by Ford and Willys-Overland were followed by over half a million standardised general purpose vehicles from 1941 to the end of the war. The Jeep had a 2.2 litre four-cylinder petrol engine developing 60 bhp, a three-speed gearbox with high or low range and disengageable drive to the front axle.*

Right: *Nikolas Straussler was a well known designer of off-road vehicles in Europe. He worked for Weiss Manfred in Hungary before bringing some of his prototypes to England, where he acted as consultant to such firms as Garner and Alvis. This is his G1 (Garner) 4 x 4 of the late 1930s with a Ford V8 engine. Similar vehicles were produced in quantity at Morris-Commercial, Guy and Fordson whilst Garner made a small number of heavier 4 x 4 lorries with twin Ford V8s.*

15

LAND-
ROVER
PROTOTYPES
IN ACTION
1947

An early compilation shot by the Rover Company showing various Land-Rovers, including the original centre-steered prototype, undergoing tests particularly to show their suitability for agricultural work.

THE UBIQUITOUS LAND-ROVER

Of the dozens of new makes of 4 x 4 that have grown up since the Second World War, the Rover Company's Land-Rover is surely the most widely known and respected. It was, though, by no means revolutionary: as has been described, in the 35 years before the Land-Rover arrived, there had been many designs that were far more sophisticated. However, what the Land-Rover had, and all but the Jeep lacked, was just the right combination of power, off- and on-road performance, ground clearance, strength, weight, carrying capacity, low price and simplicity. Virtually everything that had gone before was too expensive to be of anything but highly specialist use; whilst it may have been superior in some respects it

was ultimately let down by its cost and the difficulty of servicing it or finding spares far from the factory where it was made.

The Land-Rover was deliberately constructed to be worked on by anyone with basic mechanical skills and was initially conceived as an agricultural vehicle that a blacksmith could probably service or mend. Nevertheless, compared with the Jeep, it had, and still has, one feature in particular that places it in a category of its own. That is its aluminium alloy bodywork: this has ensured that examples have survived for forty years, even long after the paint has worn off the metal panels.

The choice of Birmabright alloy (which cost three times as much as steel but was only a third of the weight) seems obvious

A view of the Rover works at Solihull in the mid 1950s, showing the moving assembly lines full of left-hand drive vehicles for export. Note the oil cooler in front of the radiator on the vehicle in the middle foreground. These were fitted to vehicles used to power stationary equipment, such as fire pumps.

A very early example of a long-wheelbase Series I Land-Rover with capstan winch amongst the pygmies of the Ituri Forest in the Congo in 1955. The explorers are Hal and Helena Weaver. Land-Rovers soon became standard equipment for such journeys and John Baldwin, the publicity manager at Rover (and father of the author) had a collection of several dozen books describing epic journeys they had achieved.

The original centre-steered Land-Rover prototype running an elevator from its rear power take-off. This was largely a Jeep with its engine and gearbox replaced by Rover units.

in retrospect but at the time it was a decision forced on Rover by its inadequate steel allocation. In material-starved post-war Britain, where earning foreign currency was of paramount importance, motor firms were allocated steel in proportion to their previous export achievements. Rover had typically catered for the British middle classes and had sold few cars abroad. Therefore it needed to use something other than steel if it was to increase output.

The managing director at Rover since 1933, and the firm's undoubted saviour,

A view under a very early Land-Rover showing the offset differentials and a separate power take-off shaft running a belt pulley.

Sir Winston Churchill was one of many notable owners of Land-Rovers. When one was demonstrated to him at Chartwell in 1954 he insisted that the driver take it into a swamp to see what happened when it got stuck. The answer was that smartly dressed Rover directors and staff had to push it out and were showered with muddy water from the spinning wheels!

was Spencer B. Wilks, who had previously run Hillman. His brother Maurice was in charge of engineering from 1931 to 1957. Rover purchased two war-surplus Jeeps and Maurice Wilks was much impressed by their abilities, though as an engineer he was confident that they could be improved upon.

His original prototype was a mixture of Jeep and Rover parts and had a central

A long-wheelbase Series I being used for an unusual purpose, even by Land-Rover standards. It is fitted with a device for hitting golf balls to test their resilience and equality.

Before factory-built forward-control models became available Carmichael built some to its own design to accommodate its fire-fighting bodywork and equipment. The basis is a long-wheelbase Series II Land-Rover.

One of Rover's own prototypes for a forward-control 2 ton capacity military model is shown here. Various engines were tried, including the 3 litre straight six from the P5 car.

The British Royal Family have long been users of Land-Rovers. This one, built specially for ceremonial occasions, allowed the Queen to stand or sit in the rear. It was photographed before a royal occasion at Edinburgh in 1960.

For even greater cross-country ability, particularly on deeply rutted forest tracks, Roadless Traction modified this long-wheelbase Land-Rover in 1959 to take 10 x 28 tyres. It had hub-reduction axles which reduced its top speed to 30 mph (48 km/h).

21

A 1972 long-wheelbase Series III with hard top at work with the North Eastern Electricity Board in the sort of conditions in which Land-Rovers excel. The newly situated lights (in the wings instead of the grille) were a construction and use requirement. Note the front-mounted winch.

steering position, as befitted an agricultural vehicle. However, subsequent pre-production vehicles had the steering wheel moved to the side, but differed from later Land-Rovers in having a galvanised chassis and a free wheel. This latter feature overcame the transmission wind-up that inevitably occurred if front and rear wheels covered different distances (such as when turning corners) on hard surfaces. A few of the earlier vehicles had disengageable front drive and, after a couple of years, the free wheel was discontinued on the grounds that it added expense and complexity. As with the Jeep, there was a high and low range for the gearbox, though in this case four basic forward gears, giving eight forward and two reverse. The Land-Rover had an immensely strong steel chassis, designed by Olaf Poppe, that used box sections.

The Land-Rover was favourably received at the Amsterdam Show early in April 1948 and in 1949-50 eight thousand were built, over two thousand more than the number of Rover cars in the same period. Half a million were sold by April 1966, a million by June 1976 and by 1988 the total was about 1½ million, with approximately 70 per cent going for export (to more than 175 different countries over the years).

Despite its outwardly similar appearance over more than forty years of production, the Land-Rover changed substantially over this period. The Series I used the Rover 60 1600 cc engine, increased to 2 litres in late 1951. From 1955 a longer-wheelbase version was added and the original short model grew from an 80 inch (2.04 metre) to an 86 inch (2.21 metre) wheelbase in 1954 and then to 88 inches (2.24 metres). This length was standardised for the more rounded-looking and wider-track Series II of 1958, then the long Land-Rover grew from 107 to 109 inches (2.71 to 2.76 metres). A 2 litre Rover diesel had been offered since 1957 and this continued in the Series II in instances when the new 2.25 litre petrol unit was not specified. For the Series IIA the diesel was of the same dimensions as the petrol engine and there were also a forward-control 1½ ton version, heavy-duty normal-control types and all sorts of custom-converted Land-Rovers. In addition there were factory-built station wagons and specialist military types, including a V8-

engined forward-control model from 1975 and a simplified air-portable utility vehicle in service from 1968.

The Series III of 1972 onwards had various new comforts, in addition to an all-synchromesh gearbox, and could have six-cylinder and then V8 petrol engines as well as the usual four-cylinder options.

One of the Land-Rover's strengths (as well as a weakness) was its extremely rugged semi-elliptic suspension. This was retained on the grounds that, if a driver was being badly shaken on a rough track, he was likely to slow down before he could damage the vehicle. The success of the Range-Rover had shown that a more sophisticated suspension, though still with beam axles to maintain ground clearance, could answer most of the criticisms, yet still impart great strength. This coil spring set-up with double-acting dampers was incorporated in the One Ten model of 1983 and the Ninety introduced in the following year.

The Land-Rover had been produced under licence or by Rover affiliates in many parts of the world. One of the earliest versions was by former luxury car-maker Minerva in Belgium in the early 1950s, followed by Tempo in Germany. In Spain, Metallurgica Santa Ana has made Land-Rover Santana 4 x 4s since 1959, including some models not offered by the original Solihull factory. Santana also makes 4 x 4s of other origins, as befits a firm that in the 1980s became part-owned by Suzuki.

In 1970 the Range-Rover was a brave step away from the basic simplicity of the Land-Rover. Its permanent four-wheel drive required a centre differential to overcome wind-up and its height-adjustable rear suspension, long wheel travel and powerful V8 engine soon established it as a superb on- and off-road performer. It soon achieved cult status with demand vastly outstripping supply.

In 1967 the Rover Company was acquired by the expanding Leyland empire and Land-Rover production reached a record 58,000 in 1975. After that there were many world-wide problems which saw the traditional Third World markets unable to afford the typical 83 per cent of Solihull's output. Indeed in 1992 only 11 per cent went to the Third World, but meanwhile the developed countries' leisure market had expanded dramatically, partly owing to the new Discovery. Whilst this was being developed Land-Rover found itself the jewel in the crown of the potential break-up of the Leyland Group. In 1986, when a turbo diesel became available, JCB, Lonhro, Aveling-Barford, Schroder Ventures and GMC all made tentative approaches, but to keep the volume car

The Discovery in V8i three-door form and as the five-door model introduced early in 1991. The latter in this instance has a 2.5 turbo diesel engine.

Left: *At the end of 1990 two hundred examples of an ultra-luxurious 3.9 litre Range-Rover were called the CSK in honour of Charles Spencer King, who had created the Range-Rover in 1970. Here the author tries one in wintry conditions in mid Wales.*

Below: *XD 90, 110 and 130 ambulance versions of the Defender. These are part of an order of 8800 Land-Rovers for the British Army.*

section viable the government persuaded British Aerospace to acquire the whole of Rover in 1988. At that time it was estimated that 70 per cent of the 1.6 million Land-Rovers built since 1948 were still in use.

The Discovery, launched in November 1989, had sophisticated Range-Rover type running gear allied to modern styling to bridge the gap between estate cars and Japanese 4 x 4s that spent most of their time on the road. The Discovery halted Land-Rover's slipping sales and output in 1990 was the highest for fifteen years at 66,185. This was helped by Rover's own 2.5 TDi diesel that replaced the VM unit previously imported (and now used by Jeep and others). The new engine gave 25 per cent more speed and 25 per cent more torque, yet used 25 per cent less fuel. In 1994 it developed into the 111 bhp 300 TDi, though

meanwhile some Discovery models had received 2 litre T16 petrol engines as found in the Rover 800.

British Aerospace forged technical and manufacturing links with Honda and late in 1993 the Discovery was launched through the Verno dealership chain in Japan as the Honda Crossroad. From 1989 the 3.5 litre V8 used in all three types of Land-Rover was available in 3.9 litre form. The traditional 'working' models had been renamed Defender for 1991 and forty-eight of the 110 types were soon working alongside Hummers in the US Army as special operations vehicles, where their slimmer girth suited air-portability. This led to the relaunch of the traditional Land-Rover in the United States after an absence of eighteen years.

The Range-Rover was moved increasingly

The Freelander was unveiled in 1997 and in 2000 became even more versatile with the addition of a Td4 diesel by BMW and V6 177 bhp petrol versions, the latter with five-speed Steptronic transmission. The Freelander is Europe's biggest selling 4 x 4 and is due in America late in 2001.

up-market with a 4.2 litre version in the Vogue LSE of 1992. This developed 200 bhp and had electric air suspension. At the other end of the scale a 200 TDi version was driven from John o'Groats to Land's End at an average speed of 41 mph (66 km/h) with a creditable 53 mpg (18.7 km/litre) fuel consumption.

In 1994 the Discovery was launched in the United States and nine thousand Land-Rover employees were making 1200 Discoveries, 280 Range-Rovers and 470 Defenders per week. Total output was 94,716 in the year, which included part of an order for 640 Range-Rovers for Virgin Atlantic to chauffeur VIP clients.

Early in 1994 BMW acquired the Rover Group from British Aerospace for £800 million and launched a five-year £1.5 billion investment package.

Under development for years with the codename 'Pegasus', the all-new Range-Rover was launched in September 1994 with

increased space, luxury and the option of a 2.5 litre six-cylinder BMW turbo diesel. The petrol V8 engines were revised at the time in 4 and 4.6 litre versions developing up to 225 bhp for a 125 mph (200 km/h) top speed and 0–60 mph (0–96 km/h) in 9.3 seconds. The traditional style of Range-Rover lasted to February 1996, by when employment at Solihull had grown to eleven thousand (all car output having been transferred to Cowley in 1983).

In response to the massive growth in the 4 x 4 leisure market, catered for largely by Japanese manufacturers, Land-Rover unveiled its Freelander in 1997. This could be a three- or five-door machine with optional open rear quarterdeck. It was the first Land-Rover with monocoque construction and the first intended to operate primarily with front-wheel drive until loss of traction automatically introduced additional drive to the rear.

At the end of 1998 came an entirely new Discovery with self-levelling suspension, greatly decreased roll tendency and a remarkable new five-cylinder 2.5 litre turbo diesel engine. In 2000 BMW sold the Land-Rover business to Ford for three billion euros (£1.84 billion). Production of all types of Land-Rover reached 175,608 in 2000, with the 200,000 mark on target for 2001.

The evolution of the Range-Rover: the thirtieth anniversary LE is in the foreground, the LSE behind it, and the first and the last of original shape beyond. Approximately half a million Range-Rovers had been built by 2000.

Developed from 1959, and available from 1963, the Volvo Laplander or Valpen (Puppy) used the B18A 68 bhp car engine. Since the mid 1950s Volvo had made some 4 x 4 radio and command cars similar to Humbers for the Swedish Army.

THE POSTWAR JEEP AND ITS RIVALS

It was not just the Rover Company that saw scope for a Jeep-type vehicle after the war. Several other British firms toyed with the idea and the complex Austin Champ reached production for the Army. In Germany the Universal Motor Gerat appeared in 1948 and so impressed Daimler-Benz that the design was acquired in 1951 and used to create the multi-purpose Unimog.

In the United States Willys-Overland introduced its peacetime Jeep CJ series; it was taken over by Henry J. Kaiser, becoming Willys Motors Incorporated in 1952. Subsequently the Kaiser Jeep Corporation, it merged with American Motors (AMC) in 1970 and thus joined a group whose predecessors had been responsible for the famous Quad of First World War origin. AMC's Rambler division had previously supplied Jeep with its more powerful engines, though some had also come from Buick.

Just as the Land-Rover evolved from a spartan vehicle, so did the Jeep into ever more refined models that were equally at home on the highway. Jeeps have been made under licence in numerous countries, notably by Hotchkiss in France, Beijing in China, Mahindra & Mahindra in India, Viasa in Spain, Mitsubishi in Japan and even Ford of Canada for military purposes.

After a spell of Renault control from 1978, Jeep was acquired by Chrysler in 1987. In 1998 Chrysler merged with Daimler-Benz and the combined group has taken a stake in Mitsubishi and Hyundai.

As well as Mitsubishi and its version of the Jeep, Nissan made a near carbon-copy from the early 1950s, as did Toyota. Both these, and other Japanese motor firms, later developed improved designs and in the early 1970s started to tap a world-wide demand for smaller 4 x 4s, as typified by the Suzuki

LJ10 Jimny. Steyr-Daimler-Puch had been working to the same ends in Austria since 1959 with its Haflinger forward-control miniature 4 x 4, but high prices limited sales volumes. From 1985 Steyr made the G-wagen 4 x 4 for Mercedes-Benz and later added various Jeep models for Chrysler.

In the United States Jeep was challenged from 1961 by International Harvester with its Scout, and even Ford returned to the fray with first a Jeep-like MUTT military vehicle in the 1950s and then the civilian Bronco in 1965. General Motors made 4 x 4 pick-ups and estate cars from 1969 and Dodge in the Chrysler Group continued to make Power Wagons reminiscent of its wartime 4 x 4s, before developing its modern Ramcharger in 1974. With a long history of off-road vehicles, General Motors' products in the 1990s included the 5.3 litre Tahoe (available in Britain from 2000) and the Hummer, which it had adopted from a low-profile military role, as the ultimate (if somewhat impractically wide) civilian off-roader. General Motors also has important financial stakes in Isuzu, Subaru and Suzuki as well as its traditional ownership of Vauxhall and Opel and a strategic alliance with Fiat.

Numerous car firms tried their luck in the 4 x 4 field. Alfa Romeo and Fiat made examples from the early 1950s; Austin made the civilian Gipsy from 1957 when its Champ (inherited from Nuffield) had reached the end of the road. The Munga of 1955 revived 4 x 4 interest for what ultimately became VW-controlled Audi. Four-wheel drive versions of Citroens, Renaults and Peugeots were offered from the early 1950s. Numerous Russian factories built 4 x 4 utilities, military vehicles and even off-road versions of the Pobieda car in the mid 1950s. Volvo made 4 x 4 cars in the same era, followed by a fully off-road forward-control 4 x 4 from 1959. The list of models is long and includes far more names if the efforts of agricultural, military and other specialist firms like Stonefield are included. Their products range from diminutive all-terrain vehicles powered by air-cooled motorcycle engines up to enormous trucks for hauling oilfield equipment.

'Off-roading' for fun has its origins in 'trialling' with spartan cars like the Cannon in the 1950s and expanded rapidly in the 1960s as the craze for beach buggies spread from California. These 4 x 2 Volkswagen-based vehicles, mostly of American origin, had good off-road ability due, in part, to clever tyre design (which later spread to 4 x 4 vehicles). This stimulated demand for more robust vehicles from hunters, fishermen and lovers of the outdoors who wanted to get off the beaten track. 'Fun' versions of the Jeep and other American 4 x 4s met the requirements of some, but the cheaper and more compact Japanese Suzukis and Daihatsus of the 1970s opened up a much greater demand.

The Ford Military Utility Tactical Truck (MUTT) was an updated version of the wartime Jeep that was developed in the 1950s and produced from 1960 by Ford, and later by Kaiser Jeep and AM General. Ford entered the civilian 4 x 4 market in 1965 with the Bronco.

Jensen pioneered ultra-safe, high-performance 4 x 4 cars in 1965 but it was left to Audi to make a commercial success of the idea from 1980 . Quattros became rally champions; this one is taking part in the 1983 New Zealand event. After twenty years 820,000 Quattros were in use.

Jeeps of 1944 and 2000. The direct descendant of the wartime model is the Wrangler. The Cherokee (shown here is a Sport version) is far more comfortable and luxurious.

In the foothills of the Atlas Mountains of Morocco a camel train passes a convoy of Renault Mégane Scenic 4 x 4 test vehicles. The photograph was taken from the author's car.

From the 1970s Subaru made a feature of 4 x 4 for its off-road pickups. It later added general purpose off-roaders (like the 2000 Forester shown) and high-performance 4 x 4 cars, culminating in a long series of Imprezas that began in 1992.

Daihatsu entered the off-road market in 1975 with the Taft, followed in 1984 by the Fourtrak (which was also available as the Blizzard from Toyota, a firm that owned a large proportion of Daihatsu since 1966). Shown is a 1991 Fourtrak 2.8 TDX.

In 1981 Mitsubishi launched its Pajero (known as Shogun in some countries). This is a 1995 GLX five-door vehicle with a 2.8 litre turbo diesel engine. A smaller and cheaper 4 x 4 with Italian Pinin styling was later added.

As well as owning Land-Rover, Ford in 2000 offered other 4 x 4 models, such as the Ranger (shown) and the Explorer, which is claimed to be the world's best-selling 4 x 4 and is of American origin.

In the 1980s there was a marked growth in leisure as opposed to traditional off-roading and in the 1990s the trend accelerated, with British sales increasing fourfold. The various market segments increased to create new categories such as the brightly coloured compact 4 x 4s usually found coping with nothing more arduous than city streets. Then there were 4 x 4 estate cars and a new breed of highly capable premium 4 x 4s competing with the Range-Rover, such as the 5.5 litre 347 bhp 146 mph (235 km/h) version of the Mercedes M-Class. It will be joined by others, notably from Porsche-Volkswagen and Toyota's Lexus brand. The Lexus RX300 from Japan will be built in Canada from 2003.

At the other end of the scale are the compact SUVs (Sport Utility Vehicles). Sales of the Toyota RAV4 in Britain grew from 1648 in 1994 to 7492 in 1998. They subsequently fell back as new products from Suzuki and Subaru, as well as the Daihatsu Terios, Kia Sportage and Hyundai Santa Fe, came on to the market, but an all-new RAV4 was introduced for the new millennium. In the medium sector two of Land-Rover's former business partners, Honda and BMW, entered the field, whilst Nissan revised its long-established Patrol and Ford's associate Mazda joined the competition for the first time in late 2000 with its five-seater Tribute. Nissan had previously made Ford's Maverick 4 x 4 in its Barcelona factory (where the Ebro Jeep had been built in the 1960s). The Maverick is now a close relative of the Tribute. In addition to being a major importer of 4 x 4s of every sort, Britain is a major producer. As well as the obvious Land-Rover, General Motors makes all its Fronteras in Britain (21,000 in 1998 and 37,000 in 1999) and is moving production to larger facilities at Ellesmere Port in 2001. Honda sold 7660 of its CR-Vs in Britain in 1999, second in volume only to Freelander in its segment, and decided to build this model at Swindon, with 20,000 produced in 2000. Ford countered with a £130 million update of Land-Rover's Solihull facilities and £400 to £500 million per year on product development to keep it ahead of the market.

Left: *Several unfamiliar manu-facturers offered sport utilities in Britain from the 1990s. Ssang Yong from Korea employed a British stylist. The business was acquired by Daewoo in 1998. Shown here is the Tata Safari 2.0 TDI made in India by a vast conglomerate that also manu-factures trucks and rail locomotives.*

Right: *The Frontera was built at Luton from 1991 in a joint enterprise between General Motors and Isuzu. It gradually evolved into an important product of the Vauxhall-Opel group. Here a V6 205 bhp Sport tackles the Gap near Brecon, one of the most demanding of the green lanes and one that is open to vehicles only briefly in spring and autumn.*

Left: *Volvo (in Ford's portfolio since 1999) entered the 4 x 4 estate-car market in 1997 and this is its V70 Cross Country of 2000, the year in which Audi offered its broadly similar Allroad Quattro.*

CLUBS

Clubs for four-wheel-drive enthusiasts include:

All Wheel Drive Club: Public Relations Officer, Peter Burnes, 43 Balstonia Drive, Stanford le Hope, Essex SS17 8HX. Telephone: 01327 844506.

Association of Rover Clubs Limited: Mrs Caroline Flanders, 124 Crescent Drive, Petts Wood, Orpington, Kent BR5 1BE.

Austin Gipsy Register: Mike Gilbert, 24 Green Close, Sturminster Newton, Dorset DT10 1BJ.

Land-Rover Series One Club: David Bowyer, East Foldhay, Zeal Monachorum, Crediton, Devon EX17 6DH.

Land-Rover Series Two Club: Laurence Mitchell, PO Box 251, Barnsley, South Yorkshire S70 5YN.

Quattro Owners Club: Roger Galvin, 19 Cunningham Drive, Lutterworth, Leicestershire LE17 4YR.

There is a range of magazines covering 4 x 4 vehicles. These include: *Land-Rover International, Land-Rover World, International Off-Roader, Off-Road and 4 Wheel Drive, Diesel Car and 4 x 4,* plus various club publications. There are numerous books past and present on 4 x 4 vehicles available from bookshops and auto-jumbles.

PLACES TO VISIT

As well as numerous off-road trials and events organised by clubs during most weekends of the year there are the following permanent displays. These museums are believed to have 4 x 4 and related vehicles on exhibition. Intending visitors are advised to find out dates and times of opening before making a special journey.

Airborne Forces Museum, Browning Barracks, Aldershot, Hampshire GU11 2BU. Telephone: 01252 349619.

British Commercial Vehicle Museum, King Street, Leyland, Preston, Lancashire PR5 1LE. Telephone: 01772 451011.

Dunsfold Collection, Alford Road, Dunsfold, near Godalming, Surrey GU8 4NP. Telephone: 01483 200567. (By appointment only.)

Glasgow Museum of Transport, Kelvin Hall, Bunhouse Road, Glasgow G3 8DP. Telephone: 0141 287 2720.

Haynes Motor Museum, Sparkford, near Yeovil, Somerset BA22 7LH. Telephone: 01963 440804. Website: www.haynesmotormuseum.co.uk

Heritage Motor Centre, Banbury Road, Gaydon, Warwickshire CV35 0BJ. Telephone: 01926 641188. Website: www.heritage.org.uk

Lakeland Motor Museum, Holker Hall, Cark-in-Cartmel, Grange-over-Sands, South Lakeland, Cumbria LA11 7PL. Telephone: 01539 558509.

Museum of British Road Transport, Hales Street, Coventry, West Midlands CV1 1PN. Telephone: 02476 832425. Website: www.mbrt.co.uk

National Motor Museum, John Montagu Building, Beaulieu, Brockenhurst, Hampshire SO42 7ZN. Telephone: 01590 612345. Website: www.beaulieu.co.uk

Science Museum, Exhibition Road, South Kensington, London SW7 2DD. Telephone: 0870 870 4862. Website: www.nmsi.ac.uk Also at Wroughton Airfield, near Swindon, Wiltshire SN4 9NS. Telephone: 01793 814466. Website: www.nmsi.ac.uk/wroughton

Tank Museum, Bovington, Dorset BH20 6JG. Telephone: 01929 405096. Website: www.tankmuseum.co.uk

Ulster Folk and Transport Museum, Cultra, Holywood, County Down BT18 0EU. Telephone: 02890 428428. Website: www.nidex.com/uftm

Although the Discovery has changed little in appearance, it was radically transformed under the skin for 1999 with highly sophisticated suspension and transmission systems to create what is arguably the ultimate combination of on and off road capabilities.